At the End of My Walk

Poems by Claudia Cole Bluhm

BLUE LIGHT PRESS
1st WORLD
PUBLISHING

San Francisco | Fairfield | Delhi

At the End of My Walk

Claudia Cole Bluhm

Copyright ©2021 by Claudia Cole Bluhm

First Edition.

ISBN: 978-1-4218-3685-0

Library of Congress Control Number: 2020952172

Cover photo by Nan Cassady

Author photo by Susan Arndt

1ST WORLD LIBRARY
PO Box 2211
Fairfield, Iowa 52556
www.1stworldpublishing.com

BLUE LIGHT PRESS
www.bluelightpress.com
Email: bluelightpress@aol.com

TABLE OF CONTENTS

FOUND

WE ARE ALL COYOTES

THREE STEPS FORWARD, TWO STEPS BACK

THE BATHROOM AT THE RITZ

After turkey dinners at
the Woolworths counter,
we visit the fancy bathroom
at I Magnin –
just my Gram and me.

Marble walls,
hushed powder tones,
private tinkly pee.
Holding Gram's hand.
Reverent.
Wondrous.

2
Later, bathrooms at the Ritz
with friends,
wanting to be
grand, entitled,
elite.

Kind mirrors,
loving lighting,
folded tea towels –
a sort of clean
odorless smell.

You are rich.
You are beautiful.
You are good enough.

In these bathrooms
famous people pee.

Who could have just left?
Meryl Streep
Hillary Clinton
Michelle Obama
You in another life.

You are right behind them,
part of something bigger.

Now, time for tea.
Back to our table
after that backstage pass.
Listen to the harpist,
eat a crumpet,
drink in paintings, peonies,
the grand piano –
all designed to make you feel
like royalty,
or at least
a somebody.

3
The entitled voice that grew
inside my head:
Let me drive my Mercedes,
wear designer shoes, movie star sunglasses,
Chanel lipstick.

The blank canvas upon which I painted
everything I never had:
libraries, a classical education,
Persian carpets,
the tinkling of silver spoons in china teacups,
intact morals, and snow.
A revised history.

A happy ending
served on a silver platter.

The competing voice that asked
about the consequences
of the status quo?
Wasting precious time
in a land of equivocation?

If only you'd open your eyes,
the path to grandmother's house
is wide and starlit.

4
I think of Gram...
the two-year-old who traveled by train
from Brooklyn to San Francisco
just in time for the 1906 earthquake.

The redheaded clotheshorse trying on outfits
in dressing rooms with friends,
snipping out Saks labels
to sew into less fashionable attire
worn to speakeasies during Prohibition.

The best dancer in town marries a *Goy* –
my father's father,
who turns out to be a no-good
shicker – drunk.

The hard working divorcee
proud of graduating
from Katharine Gibbs Secretarial School,
raising a son on her own.

5
Every Saturday, my brother and I
clap and clamor
as Gram enters the front door –
her pillbox hat atop recently coifed curls,
creamy translucent skin.
A stole wrapped around her shoulders,
she smiles down at us as she
carries shopping bags filled with groceries,
and somewhere hidden
toys or books,
a smooth white bakery bag
filled with maple bars and jelly doughnuts
we dip in coffee and mostly milk.
Her brown eyes embers
as she leans over, kisses my cheek,
smelling of Pond's cold cream
loving me in Yiddish,
"My *sheyne meydele*."
My beautiful girl.
Crooning fairytales
in her Brooklyn accent.

Anywhere Gram stood
was home,
as safe as Heidi's Alps.

6
I'm sixteen,
in the passenger seat of Dad's Thunderbird
as he drives over the mountain road
from the beach to the city,
where I am to spend the night with Gram.
Dad says, "Since she retired, she's getting forgetful."
My feverish anguish at having to spend even one night away
from my surfer-slash-drug-dealer-boyfriend,
jealous thoughts circling like a homing pigeon.
Is he with another girl?

Gram's hands shake
as she picks up her porcelain coffee cup
from one of the doilies that seem to be everywhere.
But as she describes the big earthquake –
her family stay in an Army tent in Golden Gate Park,
I forget my boyfriend.
I want to crawl into Gram's lap.

She puts on Barbra Streisand's *Funny Girl* album,
takes my hands
and spins me around the floor,
sure-footed, laughing.

Afterwards, I curl up on her smooth white couch,
head pressed into cushions,
as she blows me kisses through the dark.

The next morning, before I hitchhike home,
I hunt through Gram's black leather purse,
stuff a twenty-dollar bill into my pocket.
I rummage through her closet,
put on a vintage white blouse with abalone buttons
hidden under my jacket.

As Gram holds onto my hand,
not wanting to let go, shame burns.
How can I steal from my Gram?

7
I'm nineteen.
Dad says, "Your grandmother was mugged by some asshole.
Has some kind of amnesia. You need to take care of her."

I hold Gram's small-boned hand
as I lead her away from the beach,
where she has gone in search of the phantom bus
she imagines will take her back to the city.
She can't place exactly who I am.
When I try to explain why she can't go home,
she starts to cry.
Our roles reversed.

During that summer
I hunt for Gram's memory,
believing it will return if we push hard enough.
Sometimes I go too far –
each morning, waking early with a start,
caught between dreams of the night before
and fear of the day ahead.

Shivering as thoughts spin out of control
along with Gram's repeated questions.

Time feels like forever –
captured in the confines of that small house
like a coffin,
waiting for my parents to return.

8
In my late twenties,
I visit Gram at the old age home.
Dad doesn't come.
"I can't stand to see her that way."

Propped in a hospital bed,
Gram's hair completely grey,
not a smile or a frown,
sunken cheeks,
dentures forgotten in a plastic cup.
The brown of her eyes faded,
staring straight ahead –
no flicker of recognition.

The delicate fingers of her right hand
repetitively pick at pieces of lint on the blanket.

Tears run down my cheeks
as I take both her hands in mine.
Gram, I'm sorry.
I loved you more than anyone.
I was so screwed up.
I've changed. I wish you could see me now.

9
After Gram died,
decades of deconstructing, reconstructing,
feeling the guilt, anger and sadness
which eventually recede.
Apologizing to Gram
forgiving my younger self,
her desperation.
Forgiving my middle-age self,
mistaking style for content –
appearances that masked inner pain.
I leave behind my Mercedes
and Ferragamo's with the staid bow
as love comes to the foreground.

10
I pull on slacks and sensible flats –
choose a colorful top
I think the second-graders will like.
Before running out the door,
I stuff *Fancy Nancy's Spectacular Spectacles*
into my bag for Surai,
a student who loves Fancy Nancy
but isn't excited about the glasses she now has to wear.
Right before I climb the steep hill
to the classroom where I volunteer,
I stop at the local bakery to pick up my low-fat latte,
and a croissant for the teacher.

That morning, in the bare-walled industrial green
elementary school bathroom,
bright fluorescent lighting casting an unflattering sheen

on paper towels with a sandpaper feel,
my voice echoes as
I show Ariana how to wash her hands
thoroughly with soap.

Sing happy birthday two times.
Make sure to get under the nails,
like this –
a precaution for COVID.

She glances up with doubtful eyes.
Let's pretend it's your birthday, I say.
We sing Happy Birthday together two times,
loud and clear
then break out laughing.

I am finally able to be a Gram.

THE MOON AND THE TIDE

Fragmented. Scattered
each in our own silos, pods,
surrounded by a million tv channels,
social media, memory clouds, iClouds.
Where are the real clouds –
white and grey set against a blue sky?
Where is the real moon –
yellow and strong, pulling our tides?

The moon and the tides
the natural rhythm of things –
new moon, crescent, waxing gibbous,
harvest moon, corn moon, strawberry moon
Not a lost moon – red and angry –
a motherless moon that has lost
her rhythm and her way.

Tides rushing in too fast,
garbage dumps in the middle of the sea,
gumming up the world with
soda cans, baggies, sinister plastic waste
lurking in the dark,
reflecting our irresponsibility in starlight.

Forest fires, orange haze and dust
apocalyptic –
the ancient word for irresponsible.
Controlled burns –
a rudder, a moral imperative
all scattered.

We scatter during the pandemic –
run underground
like panicked squirrels –
hiding, trying to save
moments of love,
remembrance of touch
like acorns.

During the fires, seeking pockets
of fresh air, a breeze, some truth,
we try to save ourselves,
maybe our neighbor,
but the world seems so vast.
We're struck by moments of gratitude,
thankful for what we have.

But also moments knowing the tides are
swirling whirlpools with depths unknown –
angry gods – this time for shooting
a young black man in his back seven times.
For not feeding the poor.
For not giving them homes and mental health clinics.

I have all this space, so many rooms.
I wander back and forth. Pace. Worry.
Holding tightly my acorns.
The moments I have loved.
I feel them slipping out of my hands,
scattered in distant tributaries.

Will we emerge, like stars in the night,
each holding a candle,
like tiny moons,
enabling the tides to find their way?

CONVERSATION WITH MY SOUL

1.
Hold my breath so hard.
Try, try and try.
Always hunched over, looking down.
I never dreamed that I could fly.

I was one of those
in the dark – hold on –
follow the wall with your hands,
wall to table to chair,
then sit – right there.

But every time the tectonic plates would shift,
I couldn't get a grip.

Torn apart,
        legs spread,
                awkward,
                        dangling –

Where's my core
        my strength
        my heart?

Lately, something is happening
a huge shift –
more on purpose
on point
not adrift.

The words just come
from somewhere
nowhere
out of control.

I don't try to hold them –
squeezed in narrow vessels
in my head.

The words seem to be coming
from my heart
instead.

They come
and then, they go.

Lights out.

And I am stuck in the room,
feeling for the floor,
for the door.

Do I stay and sit like a sitting duck?
Or is it possible to leave?

To open my heart,
to risk the light
where I am –
awkward and scrawny
exposed but curious.

I've been so bored
        so stored away
like grain in a basement –
        filmy windows
        dusty light.

I was always trying to find something
solid to stand on
usually piggybacking on someone else.

        Will you please give me a ride?
        Please?
        I can't do this on my own.

2.
I had always done it alone.

Because if it's really clear –
the loneliness,
the echoes of the abandoned heart
would frighten
almost kill.

I had to believe
that someone would come along.
Any minute
any day
at least in my lifetime
to take me somewhere safe.

That was my driving impulse,
not the cathedrals
      the rivers
      the mountains abroad.

Not the possibility of blue blue sky
      and maybe the
      promise that I could fly.

Well, maybe if I were really, really good.

3.
I grew up believing I had done something wrong.
The DNA
      flawed
      tainted
      wouldn't go away.

Bad seed
      bad blood.

I found myself wrapped up
in hold your tongue
choking
on a mortal sin,
the only sin.

Like I was the anti-Christ –
so deep and scarred
so fearful and alone
lying prone
on my back
waiting for attack.

The position from which narcissism soars.

It rises to the sky
because something has to
rise above it all
to clear a path
get the hell out of boredom and fear,
take me so far away from here.

Inflated,
rising up
beyond humdrum mortality.

Then, always at the end,
the fantasy would
start to bend
and I would drop,
tired and afraid,
landing in the same place
where I had started.

4
I never thought I would
really fly.
Just that fake fly
        get me high
        pie in the sky.

Then drop.

I tried so hard to control
my muscles,
taught like a dancer,
not twirling
but moving to a rigid beat.
More like a soldier
marching
exhausting control.

But lately, something is happening.
        I feel it –
            something lifts,

and I say,
"I want to be your friend,
even though
I have a list this long of
all the things I could
criticize."

It all falls away.

It happens again with another
and another.

Do I give in and let them join my
inner circle?

Which consists really only of
different versions of me
projected onto the screen of them
and ghostlike machinations in between?

And then it happened –
me with me.
I was berating and listing my faults
    I did this wrong
    and this
    and this.
I gained a pound.
I said the wrong thing.
I cannot gain my ground.
I lived the wrong life.
I never had children.
My voice no longer sings.

My phone just rings and rings –
    a salesman
    a creditor
    no one in my debt
    no one on my side
    no black mark I will forget.

5
And then this thought runs through me
    not a thought
    exactly –

    more of an ethereal sound
    like a tiny shoulder sitting fairy.

    Forgive.
    Forgive.

As corny as the Don Henley song,
profound as a sunrise,
alien as so much light.

> *Forgive. Forgive.*
> *You are one of them...*
> *In the human race...*
> *Mistakes okay...*
> *What it means to live.*

I hear these signals just barely.
They come from far away,
not quite embodying the body
      the human
      the heart.

But the whispers are
      a start.

I want to cry –
not exactly sure why
but it is such a relief
to think there might
be a way
not out – but in.

The secret just may be

> *Forgive*
> *Forgive*

      Me!!!

Is it ok?
Is it heresy – blasphemy?
Will the world run
        out of control?

Murders, shootings, stabbings.

How will I be safe?
in a moonbeam
lying on a leaf
covered by a rose petal?

What about the guns?
        The cannons?
        The danger?

We always need our weaponry
        our rapier tongue
        to punish
        to persecute
        to flatten
        to stifle
        to drain.

The words
come up like a geyser now –
energy and light.

        I can't stop them.
        They are here
        to help me through my fright.

Forgive – yourself
Forgive – your friend
Forgive – your enemy.

Stand tall.
No need to hide your stomach
your wrinkles
your secret affairs
(after all, they were only in your head.)
Your lists of mistakes
you've turned to
       crimes
       against
       humanity.

Bad bad girl.

       Forgive – she says – not in a hiss
       or a sing song voice.
       Not in a cultish way.
       Not like a cover tune,
       no manipulative sway.

It sounds like a painting,
the one in the London Gallery –
the Da Vinci with the halo,
Madonna and child.
This is wild! How can it be?

The mother and the baby
are both me.

In genuine affection
saying:

It's okay
I'm sorry

We all make mistakes
I love you

I know
you love me.

My confidence builds.

I know you would never try to hurt me.
Forgive?

Forgive.
Let's go.
Let's live.

Let's fly.

CHILDHOOD

LIBERTY STREET

I've walked Tennessee Valley three times since it opened up last Monday. The trail has grown so lush and green during its Covid hiatus – nothing trampled. Bunnies scurry across the path. The trail ends at a beach, where I put my bare feet and hands into the surf and felt like I cleansed months of antibacterial disinfectant – the cold saltwater a salve for all the compulsive handwashing and my chapped psyche. For moments, I almost felt free.

When I was maybe six – seven – eight years old on Liberty Street in San Francisco, I felt a kind of freedom. Probably too much for that age – what would now be called unsupervised. It was more of a norm then. On rooftops four stories up, hopping over back-yard fences, roaming blocks and blocks away from home.

I knew the inside of every Victorian on our post-WWII block. From the Scottish Catholic Callaghans next door and their ten kids who went to Most Holy Redeemer and wore uniforms and whose house always smelled like haggis and cabbage. Across the street, the Franz's, who had escaped the Nazis. Their grandson, Robert from London, who visited during the summertime and spoke with a British accent.

The Azevedos – the nightclub singer dad who spoke Spanish, slept late and walked around in boxer shorts, and his Irish wife, Molly, who wore colorful muumuus. And their beautiful children – two girls who all the boys had crushes on. The older one won dance prizes on American Bandstand; the younger one, a singer just like her dad; and two boys who all the girls had crushes on.

The Puerto Rican family down the street were cousins of the

SF Giant's first baseman, Orlando Cepeda, who played basket-
ball with the kids when he visited and once brought over Willie
Mays. The Czechoslovakian single mom with her daughter, a
classmate who had long braids and only three fingers on each
hand from thalidomide. I remember holding her hand during
folk dancing in school and trying not to notice. The German
Lutheran Werths, who took me to church, where I sang O Tan-
nenbaum in German – much to my Jewish father's dismay. My
shiksa mother thought it was hilarious.

I was always going to church, believing I needed to be redeemed
and save my family from hell and the fire that burned forever.
That was June Callaghan's influence. "Yer father's a Jew; you can
tell by his nose. Yer gonna go ta hell." Obsessed with rosaries, I
stole one from June Callaghan's older sister Marie's dresser. Marie
never noticed, maybe because she had moved on to the making-out-
with-boys stage. Patsy Callaghan and I would spy on Marie and her
beaus kissing on the living room couch through a keyhole.

There was Linda Avila – I think her father was Spanish. One
day, she poured catsup on her younger sister in the basement
and made me cry when she told me it was blood, and her sister
was dead. And the Irish Kilkarneys at the corner of Liberty and
Castro Street. The older boy hung out with Eddy Mullens, who
took me up to their fort on Billy Goat Hill and showed me how
to play strip poker when I was eight.

I don't remember the name of the people who lived in the house
where the parents were never home – also on Castro near Liber-
ty. Where all the big kids gyrated to 45 rpm records and made
out all over the house after school. Where Denise Choroski and
I jumped on the double bed in what must have been the parents'
bedroom. One of the older boys took Denise and me down to

the basement once and showed us a dead kitty in the freezer. We both screamed. He later joined a gang and was arrested for murder.

Frankie and his parents lived on the corner. He was from the deep South and always said, "Bless your little pea pickin' heart," which my Dad said was like Ernie Ford.

I often walked home after school with Maria Santiago, whose tongue click-clicked when she talked about her Grandma Guadalupe from Mexico who had recently died. Maria opened the door to her flat with a key she wore around her neck. Once, she led me down a dark hallway to a framed photograph of her Grandma hanging on the wall. She looked like Snow White, encased in glass with radiant blue eyes, rose tint around her lips and cheeks, and a yellow glow around her dark hair. Maria told me to watch for the eyes in the photo to move – that was how her grandmother would speak to her from the beyond. We waited and waited, and when I finally saw the eyes move, chills ran down my arms. I figured Grandma Guadalupe must be a saint.

I went to Most Holy Redeemer Church with Patsy Callaghan and read the story of Saint Bernadette in her Catechism book so many times I knew it by heart. *Saint Bernadette of Lourdes, who was downtrodden, poor and sickly, who went back and back to the Grotto to see the vision every day, even when no one believed her.* I knew all the facts about the saints: how long they had been buried before their bodies were discovered, always in miraculously preserved condition years later. I knew how beautiful they were and how much God loved them. I lengthened my name to Claudia Denise Ann Marie Sarah Bernadette Kolsch to keep myself from going to hell. But I had never heard anything about moving eyes.

I also went to church with the Cassadys, who were Unitarian. Their daughter Nan became my best friend. Her father, who always had neighbors over to discuss politics, was wrongfully accused of being a Communist. Her mother let us help make blackberry pies from scratch. Nan and I always got into trouble – mostly for laughing. We burst out giggling when Mrs. Cassady pointed out the artistic aspects of nude bodies in paintings and couldn't keep ourselves from cracking up in church.

The Cassadys lived next door to the French Trelauns, who I didn't know because they didn't have little kids. Sometimes I played with Fern Karpilow, a classmate who lived around the corner. Her parents were artists. Fern had little sisters, and I watched Fern's mother like a hawk to learn how to change diapers. She was always teaching us things. Their house always smelled sweet – like crayons and apples. They were Jewish from Brooklyn, New York – just like my Gram.

I babysat for the ballet dancers who lived in a flat on the corner of Liberty and Castro Street. I imagined they were Russian because my ballet teacher, Mrs. Parks at The Academy of Ballet, said Russians were the best dancers – but I don't think the couple on the corner were really Russian. I would steal cookies from their cookie jar while their infant slept. I didn't babysit long – just while the parents went to the store. I always seemed to be babysitting, although how anyone could leave an infant with an eight or nine-year-old – even for ten minutes – is beyond me.

The red house three houses down from us was where beatnik families moved in and out. I got my first kiss from Matt Stahl when I was six or seven years old, up in my parents' walk-in closet when his mother and mine were downstairs having coffee. When the Stahls moved out of the red house, the Hilders moved in. I played with the Hilder children, whose parents were permissive and didn't make their toddler Julia wear a diaper. The Hilders were really worried about a nuclear war and introduced me to Peter Paul and Mary – who became my new religion after I decided Christ was a hoax like Santa Claus and rosaries were just glass beads. During nuclear drills, when we hid under our desks at school around the time of the Cuban Missile Crisis, the Hilders and PP&M's songs seemed to make more sense.

After my Tennessee Valley walk, I started thinking about all this – trying to remember a time when I felt free – but what occurred to me was all the immigrants I grew up with in San Francisco. I remember my Dad talking about his whole *mespucha*, his family, and how he came from a long line of Russian peasants who fled pogroms. He said even in his generation in San Francisco's Jewish Fillmore District, the buddies he went to school with were Italians, Irish, Jews, Greeks, Negros... All sorts of ethnic names – in his generation – and mine.

We are a nation of immigrants. And as difficult as my childhood may have been at times, I miss the tapestry of Liberty Street, as good and free and refreshing as sinking my toes into the cold saltwater at the Tennessee Valley beach.

SLEEPWALK BIRTH

The operating room spins
as I imagine it.
Your legs widespread,
you look dead.
You didn't need to pant –
etherized upon the table.

Out I came
plaintive plea.

> *Help, this is an accident.*
> *This isn't my destination*
> *I should have landed*
> *a crooning song awaiting –*
> *a celebration.*
> *Where's the celebration?*

It was a sleepwalk birth,
one you don't remember.
Some say it never happened
on that shortest day of December.
Those that say it didn't
can't see me
          look sideways,
                    look through me
perpetuate my invisibility.

Those that say it happened –
there are only a few –
the main one who didn't, of course,
being you –
try to revive me
      buoy me
            get me to breathe –
implore:

> *Look in the mirror.*
> *You are a symphony.*
> *You were conceived.*
> *Breathe, damn it, breathe.*

I wanted you to hold me,
adore me,
in that event that happened so long ago
in gray light just before dawn.
You lost your childhood,
your chance to be in Hollywood.
I lost my childhood,
the chance to be a cherub.

Now I pad my way back
in unending sessions of analysis
relentlessly on the attack –
hungry for blood
waiting for catharsis.

Dawn is bleak
near the beaker on the counter,
the stethoscope that says I am alive
that says you are asleep
        you are asleep
                asleep.

WHEN I GROW UP

Early evening.
My twenty-four-year-old mother carries me upstairs,
sits me down on beige wall-to-wall carpet
as she pulls on black velvet toreador trousers,
steps into black satin sling back heels –
one of the outfits my father bought her.

She primps in front of the mirror,
putting on red lipstick.
She smiles a big sexy smile at her image,
then pats her lips with Kleenex.

Sometime after dark,
my mother's smile, wide and eager,
my father comes home.
The doorbell rings as guests arrive.
Music plays on the phonograph –
sometimes African, sometimes Greek,
sometimes Yiddish, sometimes Sinatra.

I fall asleep listening to rising sounds
of voices, laughter,
the tingling of ice in glasses –
the excitement my mother loves.

Drifting off, eyes closed, my lullaby:

> When I grow up
> I want to be pretty
> just like mommy.
> I want to wear a black taffeta dress
> and black high heels
> and hold my cigarette

just so
just the way she does.
I want to have blonde hair
and put on red lipstick
and blot it into the Kleenex
just so
just the way she does.
I want to look in the mirror
and pat my hairdo
puff puff puff
just so
just the way she does.

When I grow up
I want to marry someone like daddy,
a man who is funny and makes everyone laugh –
the life of the party.
I want someone like daddy who will let me
bounce on the bed as much as I want
and won't make me go to school
when I have a stomachache.

When I grow up
I want my daddy to think I am prettier
than anyone.
I want his eyes to light up
when he looks at me
and say, "This is my princess,
my only little girl.
who I love more than anything in the world."

That was all I wanted.

I NEVER LIE ON PURPOSE

I hear the past in too many voices –
moving from city to suburb to town,
from lower to middle class,
then finally down
to rented furniture.

My brother and I just held on
until it was over.

When we moved to the beach,
to the house with rented furniture,
Dad said it was only temporary,
but we knew he'd sold our furniture
when he'd drunk himself into some deal
in some bar with one of his other women.
My father was a thief that way.

In our family,
the outlines were always sketchy.
No one ever arrived on time,
and they always stayed late.

Each night the battle began:

The sliding glass door opens, and our father,
faltering on the aluminum railing,
bangs it shut, punctuated by *goddamn door*.
Already sarcastic from a long lunch of bourbons,
he goes for the bottle on the kitchen countertop,
red faced and clumsy,
like a dog rummaging through

a garbage can. If we were lucky, he'd just
go to his room and pass out. Usually, though,
there was a sunset period, where he blazed and flickered,
giving a speech about how selfish and undeserving we were.

Then our mother would chime in,
her wine glass filled and filled,
until her words slid, slurred
and ended up overturned on the floor.
Then, our father would fire at our mother –
two tangled voices painting the room.

My brother and I heard
anguished screams about late rent, infidelities,
unpaid bills, plumbing that wasn't fixed.
The stench of two souls battling in hell.
I wished they were dead.

I can't tell you how it really is,
but I'm still holding on –
most times nervously awake.
I lie in bed
listening to the ocean
trying to find
solid ground inside myself.

It feels so good
when I can find my way home,
and I never lie on purpose.

THE FATHER COMPLEX

INVISIBLE STRINGS

Daddy sees through his looking glass, honey.
He sees sideways, that's all.
Different.

He covers the room with a syrup –
deadly, hypnotic, seductive.

The inherent paradox of the alcoholic: the manipulation.
They pull you in,
then push you out.
Life for our family was a carnival of
my father's unexpected pushes and pulls.

He would take me in with his warmth, his humor,
push me out with his sarcasm, his anger;
take me in with his sorrow, his need,
push me out with his fire, his alcohol breath;
pull me in with baited remarks, clever words
push me out with broken promises, late rent;
pull me in with "I need you honey; you're more important than
   anyone;"
push me out with his overwhelming grip
like a dying man going down.

The irregular heartbeat of his days and nights
comings and goings,
strings attached.
I couldn't do anything on my own –
always the invisible pulling on my innermost places.
In, in like the tide not stopping;
out, out like the stars unreachable.

Twisted feelings:
the love pulled me in,
the hate pushed me out.
I tried to catch up to the love.
Always running, like you.
Always running to catch something.
Maybe you know what it is;
I don't.
I run in imitation.

The boundaries between us blurred.
Never ending images made me dizzy.
The family of empty glasses, empty hearts.

Days go by.
Nights go by,
Years go by.
My distortion grows weaker with time,
but your world still beckons.
Sometimes, I almost miss it.

PRISONER

1
I sit at a long
brass plated bar,
my twenty-nine year old
lined face repeated
in rows of mirrors.
I feel my father laughing at
my performance.

> *I remember him*
> *pacing*
> *in dim cobweb light,*
> *just outside*
> *my bedroom door.*
> *I was afraid*
> *to leave my room.*

The man next to me
hangs over
the edge of his barstool.
Clever words,
warm, smooth voice,
familiar,
clogged at the place
where sincerity is born.
I become his
for the night –
secretly searching
a way out.

He becomes my guard
feeding me scraps
of recognition
I hoard in my pocket
like gold.

> *In darkness*
> *my father stumbles up the walkway,*
> *reaching like a*
> *blind man*
> *for the sliding glass door.*

> *He has just come*
> *home from a bar,*
> *his slick good looks,*
> *mocking brown eyes,*
> *sarcastic laughter*
> *between coughs;*
> *the end of his cigarette*
> *held tight between his lips.*

> *I slam the freezer door shut,*
> *ready to escape*
> *but I am caught:*
> *"Stop eating ice cream, bubble butt."*

> *As his words*
> *ricochet across the room,*
> *I dive under and over them.*
> *We are in a war.*
> *I wait for him*
> *to pass out*
> *so I can breathe.*

2
Kidnapped,
I remain his.
I can never escape.

The scraps of
any man's
recognition
always turn into ammunition.
In my attempt
to gun them down,
I fall.

This game is fatal.

EXCUSES

A realization comes to me in a daydream: I'm surrounded by
light. Not sunlight with vital energy shining down on round-
eyed yellow sunflowers and rose vines climbing up to the heavens
like a feminine version of *Jack & the Beanstalk*. But light that's
cheap and harsh – the kind you'd find inside a windowless, dusty
bar in the middle of the afternoon.

Light that hits me in the eye, trying to tell me something: that I
am like my father.

The one way to sum up my father's life – if you strip down
the positives: looks, charm, Jewish humor, a winning way with
words. And the negatives: verbally abusive, a womanizer, an
alcoholic con. If you take all that away, there he is – naked before
God and mankind – and me, his daughter. He was a bullshitter.

Everything he never did and everything he ever did had An Excuse. I
could name a few. The time our family moved to a rental after he
sold all our furniture. He told us, "It was in storage. We weren't
using it anyway." The summer I took care of his mother – my
gram – and my father didn't come home for days, his voice in
that faraway phone booth, which I later learned was across the
street from a young chick he was *schtupping*. "Got a flat tire."
"My car's in the shop." "Can't make it over the mountain road."

His perpetual plans to make big money that I would later try to
explain:

"He didn't know how."
"He was never taught the steps to get from A to Z."
"He didn't have a father to teach him."

My excuses, for him.

In this daydream state, which comes over me like a nerve wracking revelation, I wonder, how much of me is the same? How much of me is *I'm not to blame?*

In my daydream, we are sitting together at the bar. He's as old as me. I'm as old as him – bullshitters are always the same age.

He's telling the story of how he was the best broad jumper in high school – heh – heh – heh. How he married the broad who had the best pins in town. How some scheme or other *almost* worked out. But because of this or that slight insignificant blurry – he can't quite put his finger on it – fact that changed the outcome, it didn't work. Like maybe he couldn't sit still long enough. He had to have a drink to calm himself down, get himself up, gain faux confidence, make him funny or smart.

But I'm different, I say, afraid to turn to my reflection in the mirror, trying to ignore the fact that I, too, want to look good: clean the scene, make it pristine. Cinderella Good Girl makes a mistake or two, but we all know she is *really* a Fairy Princess.

The things *I* start but never finish. Because I get lost in my head. Can't get the confidence. Too afraid. Can't settle my nerves. Just like him. But, but... *I'm not like that!* He may have seduced everyone with hilarious stories at parties, but each night his words ricocheted off the walls of our house in tantrums, rages, arguments.

This is the piece I need to isolate, dislodge, go after with the sure

49

hand of a surgeon – slice it the fuck out. The part of my brain where the circuits repeat: *I had no time. I had to help my father. He needed me. I have to help my boss. You know, make a living.*

I've got excuses lined out the door.

That insistent voice: *Maybe the apple doesn't fall far from the tree. You still haven't landed in the place where sincerity and commitment are born. What about – you know. The part you aren't feeding – you know – the soul?* Like you don't sing for months at a time and your voice wells up inside like a preacher – like a singer— fuck, like Aretha Franklin or Joni Mitchell. It grows like that – these images – and all of a sudden you are living in fantasy – because you don't feel good enough. Because your natural breath is stifled, shut down. Repressed. Regressed. Sitting on itself. Choking.

And when it finally comes out, the sound of your voice is so flimsy that you don't recognize it as yourself. You don't love it. You don't even like it. In fact, you abhor that tiny snivelly voice that sounds like – anyone else but me.

When I drove my dad to the emergency room the night he died, he put on perfectly pressed chinos, a never worn shirt, stuffed a pack of Camels in his pocket. He was so used to being fueled and fucked up for so many years on bottles of Jim Beam that even an electrolyte imbalance that would kill any normal human didn't faze him. This would be one of the most heroic feats of his life. Getting down the stairs, into the car beside me, talking like everything was fine. He said, "You and your brother – you appreciated me in the end." On the freeway driving straight ahead as fast as I could, I held his hand.

As sad as I am remembering that last night, my regrets for him, for me, for his life, for mine at that point, I can't help but won-der if I too will go out looking good – fancy pants, Ferragamo shoes, regretting my lack of instincts, the wasted time.

I see a similarity. A way of avoiding responsibility. Of knowing who I am and dancing to it. Okay, what am I trying to say? That for all my hard work, there is still bluster, banter, excuse after excuse. To not finish or stand tall.

Truth be told, I'm much stronger than the people I kowtow to – names anonymous. But I bow. I crumple. I make myself so very small, into a tiny ball.

The narcissistic mirror is what I feed them for dinner. The reflect back. The kiss kiss (kiss ass). The I'm taking care of you.
This is where I get into danger. The fraud. The deceiver. I'm hanging up my own receiver. But wait!

Will I get out of this with love? With acceptance? With for-giveness? All positive things I'm supposed to use to diffuse the negative – to overpower it? To make it fade?

Or do I call a spade a spade?

I'm on a barstool, sitting with my dad. He told me stories and was the role model I had. I'm still waiting for him to apologize. To look me in the eye and tell me that he was, in fact, as shallow as what came through. Fear transmuted to narcissism. Should I really give a fuck?

But I do. I loved him because he made me laugh. I loved him because he was mine. But beyond that, there was nothing that made him, as a father, really shine.

I need to say
I'm sorry.
I'm sorry, Dad, but I must go.
Not only because of people and places I have to see
But because the birds of paradise are waiting all in a row.
Time.
Time.
Time.
Together we have wasted more than our share.
Wish me well.

I need a ritual to allow me to leave.
To really go –
nothing up my sleeve.
No excuse
Not one.
To try to get you back –
like a lover
like a lost puppy.
My daddy
who reeled me in
again and again.
I tried to push him out
and make myself real.

Today I pledge
to make myself real.

Don't be fooled
by the fools
on the barstool
or anywhere else.

Even in Nirvana,
if they have an excuse –
if they say,
"Sorry, I couldn't make it.
I had a flat tire."

Turn your back
And walk away.

THE MOTHER COMPLEX

IN THE MIDDLE OF THE NIGHT

Your pale blue eyes,
blond fine hair,
wisps of smoke
from your cigarette,
always against a background
like a distant horizon.
My mother is foreign to me,
lost somewhere
over the edge of the earth.

In the middle of the night,
I wake up in my bed –
my blanket
the last vestige of you.
I am desperate
terrified
of never having what I never had.

If I let go now,
what will there be?
No shred of evidence
that you existed at all.

Now I worry.
Will you drink yourself
into high blood pressure,
violent and spattering?
Will you lose your job?
Will you finally forget me –
the last straw.
Or did that happen first?

Will you never hold my hand
as we walk down the beach?

If I don't let you go,
I will go under too.

If you keep drinking
like that, you'll die
or will I?

You're dying now
I'm dying too.

The longer I let this go on,
the older I get,
the more I become your mother.
You are as an infant,
helpless.
How can I let you
lie there in so much pain?

If I really believe
I can't save you,
why do I keep coming back?

Lately, you are a ghost –
sitting at my breakfast table
at night by my bed.
Wherever I go
you are there.

Do I exist without you?
Do I exist at all?

You are ruining
my dream:

> We live in a house
> sunny and light.
> You keep me warm
> and kiss me each night.
> You are always there
> when I'm afraid.
> You teach me lessons,
> so I'm well prepared
> for life.

MIND LIKE A STEEL TRAP

1
Frantic
to catch time in my net,
as if there is one moment
I cannot forget,
and I don't even know what it is.

How to stop time?
How to control it,
to change the order of things,
to become omnipotent as kings
think they are?

Where does it go?
Where do I?

The pain of getting lost
in your blue blue eyes,
that blue blue sky
that seems to go on forever,
but really must have a limit
like life, right?

I will miss you when you go
I already do.
I'm not choosing for myself
anything but a place
inside your heart
that eludes me still.

2
This morning you could not remember
your address.

The one thing we have always had –
your mind.
My mother has a mind like a steel trap
on which I rely
as if it were her love.

If you forget
as you fade into vague,
does that mean you will never
love me?
If logic fails,
what then?

Underneath the vast unconscious,
I am not sure you know
or I know
if you are capable
of love.

Would your first impulse be
like the time when I was five?
I showed you how bears kissed,
"Like this mommy!"
Giggling, I slapped you
and you slapped me right back.

Would your first impulse be
to have a drink?
Is that the last thing
you would remember?

3
Like Dad
on his final trip to the hospital –
he stuffs a brand new pack of Camels
into his shirt pocket,
ready for anything
ready for death.

No rosaries in this family
no *yamachas*
no prayer bowls
no lighthouse.

I wish your mind like a steel trap,
your high IQ
would encompass
me
would caress my heart,
wrap around it.

Instead,
I am caught in the woods
on my way to grandmother's house.

I got lost;
you got lost.
We are lost together.

But when I hold onto your
strong symmetrical logic,
even the harsh punctuation,
I feel held
in a space that is
smooth, cold, like a shelf.
It is me alone, and no one else
shares you there.

4
What is the capital of Italy?
The square root of 359?
You know the myths of the Greeks,
how to speak Latin,
the history of avalanches,
forest fires.

You majored in the history of the world.
You are my history.
You were my world.

You know Europe like the back of your hand.
I was so afraid to fly.
When I finally landed
in Paris at age 42,
I found a part of you.
Was it your heart?

You recommended we stay
on Il St. Louise
next to Notre Dame.
I loved
the way it scaled the sky.

"Is that my mommy?"
I asked as I looked up.

5
I imagine what it will be like
when you go.
Will you leave something behind?
Have you already?

If I go inside the cathedral,
sit in a pew,
is that wine I smell?
Sweat, sex, men,
bars?

No, can't be!
I'm in a church,
a cathedral – Notre Dame
which I change to
Half Dome in Yosemite.
After all
they are the same –
monuments to God
or whatever is behind
the mystery.

As I sit in warm springs
near a waterfall,
I contemplate
you
your mother
the Mother of us all.

6

Your mama does love you
in her own way –
the way of the steel trap mind,
the way of the heart trapped in
the steel trapped mind.

Together you love
to read Harry Potter,
a good cup of coffee
the plants on her veranda
the cathedrals
the fantasies they bring
and, ironically, the belief in no heaven.

Places we intersect,
sit together
roles reversed –
now mother, now daughter.

It brings back all those years
ironed flat like napkins,
where we waited together,
my mother and I,
for my father to come
for our lives to change.

We waited for someone to tell us
what to do,
for someone
to warm the cold
places in our hearts.

How much this remembering
makes me want
a cathedral sized
Half Dome sized
hug.

FOUR A.M.

In Memory of Jocelyn

I hear a voice.
Do you hear it too?
Is it the rumbling of the earth?
Is it the rustling of a breeze?
Is it you?
A place you are coming through?

Is it the beginning of a thought
at the end of the day?
A reminder that you
have slipped away?

We all saw it coming.
No one knew what to do.
No one knew how to
pull you back.

Repetition of your mother's dance.
Your first steps
never gave you a proper chance.

Other girls in black patent leather
with buckles, straps and bows.
You danced in red shoes –
marked
for what reason no one knows.
You could not take them off.

A young wolf cub
tracking its mother.
A child
who knew no other.
Trance-like,
you followed.

I hear a voice –
are you telling me you're okay?
How to live and how to die –
is there a right way?

I'll always love you,
a mystery
I could not reach.

There were dozens
calling
calling to you –
"Come back, our child."
"Come back, our friend."
"Come home."

I hear a voice.
Is that what called to you?
The strongest whisper
a time
a place
a mother's promise unfulfilled?

An I-owe-you –
for that
you killed.

The unsteady flame
flickered
even less.

I wish I believed in something
instead of asking,
was I –
were we –
somehow remiss?

For that is the dance
of the red shoes –
the place that had you trapped.

Some things I will never know,
held close beside my heart.
To lose those we love –
that is the hardest part.

I climb up my cedar tree
where the view is so magnificent
for all the world to see.

Sleep, Jocelyn, sleep
held in loving arms
wake up smiling, content
in the event
you are there somewhere.

I speak
only a part
in the larger jigsaw
of your heart –

what you saw
what I see.

We all go about our business
day to day
night to night
each in our own way
each in our own sight.

We hold you
in our hearts
in our words,
our very fragile soaring bird.

LOST

THE HOMELESS MAN

Every night
the homeless man,
his back against the wall of the taqueria
on College Avenue in Berkeley,
perched or slumped,
supplicant with his paper cup for spare change.

His expression doesn't give anything away –
his intelligence, his character, what he is feeling
what year it is.

When did he disappear?

Was it in attempts to trace himself back,
block out years in between
the time he hid under the bed
making dust snowballs.
Or in a corner,
silence piercing his soul?
Or was it loud arguments,
leaving him forever meek, rolled over,
turned in on himself?
Playing dead?
Really dead.
What is the difference?

The mind of a child holding so tenaciously
onto nothing. Crying inside.
Wanting so badly to be held.
To sing along with someone.
To be next to that heartbeat,
strong and steady.

The first death long before
adolescent rage,
alcohol or drugs.
Maybe he enlisted and had to kill.
Maybe he couldn't kill.

As he sits
I wonder where does he go?
Does he travel well-worn neuron synapses?
Does he stay in the present?
Does he see me?
What happens when he has to pee or defecate?
When he's hungry
Or lonely?
Does he ever just want to talk?

Should I slip him a fiver,
as my father would say.

One day I asked him what he wanted to eat.
After a long silence, looking away,
he answered.

"Turkey on white bread.
Extra mayo.
Hold the lettuce and tomato.
No onions."

"Do you want a coffee?"

"Never drink it. Orange juice."

"Okay."

That was twenty-five years ago.
I wonder where he is now.

SUMMER IN THE CITY

For the first time since the pandemic,
I drive down Ellis Street in San Francisco,
past Glide Memorial in the Tenderloin –
faces, bodies
angular, soft
running, walking, sitting
splayed upon the sidewalk
zigzagging through cars
stopping traffic.
One man jumps on the hood
of a truck in front of me.

Long lines of despair.
Food alongside feces
on the sidewalk,
in the street.

I want to see them as people –
not as a hoard
or inmates of a boundaryless,
outdoor mental institution –
an emergency ward.

I can take one at a time,
like the must-have-been-schizophrenic guy
who recently stood in front of our house
blasting a hose in the middle of the night
flooding the basement.

When I peered down from the deck
and asked him to please leave, he said,
"I will, but first can you tell me your name?"
Then he spewed loud and angry words
I could not understand.
With wiry strength, he ran off
with our heavy hanging planters
into the night.

Or the woman who screamed
I'm gonna kill you bitch
while she ran after me
and hit me over the head.
Ambulance, police report, never to be found.

But here,
I feel outnumbered
as the souls rise up
out of summer dust
crying to be born.

SHRINE OF SHOES

1
New Year's Day.
I finally tackle
my shrine of shoes.

Pulled down from closet shelves,
they surround me on the oakwood floor.
Center stage, like royalty,
my family of Ferragamo's
in matching red boxes
with names like
Gabriella, Desideria, Lillaz, Louvre.

I eyed my first pair in college
on a Junior League debutante who
spoke fluent French and never dropped acid.
I bought my first – sleek and black –
when I joined the business world
to hide my hippie poet,
convinced she was no good.

Time to buckle down.

2
At four, I had played in my mom's walk-in closet
magical land of grown up clothes.
Outfits my father bought her –
slick sheens, soft cashmeres in smart grays and blacks,
toreador velvet pants, halter tops,
costumes, really.
Striped satin shoes in sassy colors.
One day I tried on the most beautiful light blue
kid-leather pumps, so many sizes too big
I fell down the back steps.

At six, my first important shoes –
black patent leather Mary Janes,
straps worn back like grown-up flats
with my black and white striped dress,
red apron's bow tied in back.
I was such a good girl, my muscles froze.

Act the part of the child –
never wild
never angry as you really are.
What's up with this?
Boring clothes, boring shoes
I'm bored, bored, bored.
I want science
mud, math, spiders –
dark to match
my pistol rage.

Where is my horse?
My mechanical bench?
My weight to throw around?

But I loved my dolls,
or thought I did.
I played with them,
despite Chatty Cathy's limited vocabulary.
Then there was Pollyanna –
blonde hair, blue eyes
a little too true blue
don't you think?
And the nun doll, a gift from my
gay uncle who loved Christ,
priests and religious relics.

June Callaghan next door
on Liberty Street
in her Scottish brogue,
"Yer father is a Jew.
You can tell by his nose.
Yer gonna go ta hell
and sit in the fire that burns forever."

Set me up with a place
for all pervasive guilt
to repair in the dark.
Sequester the monster in me,
that stifled roar.

In pink ballet slippers
I danced the saint under
the halo that shone above –
that glow I now perceive as neon slime
a cheap trick to keep me on the wrong track.

3

At eight, bare feet
under hospital sheets –
pageant of pain
I did not understand.
They whispered tumor.
They whispered worry.
I imagined death.

IV's, blood dripping, tocks ticking,
missed a summer, missed a year.
I could care less what shoes I wear.
Get me out of here!
I want savage feet – thick, dark, tough –
not this prissy can't play
stitches all down my side.

Sit in my window with
Chatty Cathy, Pollyanna, and Porcelain Nun dolls
making up plays.
Please mommy, please daddy – anyone.
I'm a poor unmerciful sinner.
I would rather be dead.

Oh come on!

Play acting as I lay in bed,
invisible safe in my wall
clicked to the left, clicked to the right.
I pulled out my savings
and gave it away
to classmates – to anyone
who could see
I was beautiful and about to die.

4

The wild child moccasins
I wore on my sixteenth birthday
with the hand sewn purple paisley top.
Scared out of my mind
as my stoned boyfriend
took each curve over the steep mountain road
on the way to the Jimi Hendrix concert.
Underneath hip leather
my feet quivered
shivered.
The high platform fuck-me shoes
of my twenties
when I stuck out my ass,
thinking that was the position from which
to fall in love.

Oh dear, what was I thinking?
Who was I then?
But still, I miss those shoes
Buried, thrown away, with all that promiscuity.

Where are the snakeskin rock star shoes
with pointed toes?
Witch shoes, potent – powerful.
I gave them away.

And what about the cowboy boots
from the Neil Young days
when I sang and played guitar?
Those restless shoes
that went to bars,
those long lost shoes –
why miss them?

5
Those first Ferragamo's.
Black pumps with the staid bow.
I stuffed my toes into survival mode
and hid.

Nothing dark there,
no secrets.
No slimy back-story ready
to leak out at the slightest provocation.
No creativity throbbing within –
a tiny bomb in my chest
like a terrorist
ticking to wreak havoc on the
orders swallowed daily
from men in suits.

I wanted to make enough money
so that I could let go and fuck –
be an artist,
but it was never enough.
My boss wanted my artist
working in his stead
to create imagination in his head.
Too afraid to stake my claim,
I disappeared, then blamed
and watched time pass.

6
Those first black Ferragamo's
worn with Ellen Tracy because I couldn't afford Chanel
dark Navy blue suits to suck up the sweat
pooled under my arms,
caused by rampant fear of venture capitalists.
Oh hell – who am I kidding?
Of my father
the alcoholic who ridiculed
so long and consistently I couldn't live without it.

Browbeaten into submission?
Submit
Submit
Might as well make money at it.

As my net worth slowly grew,
so did my penchant for pumps
heels higher, bows broader,
materials more exotic.

But none as precious as the first,
which I wore to my father's funeral
with a tailored black jacket and white gabardine slacks.
Symbols of respectability,
trying to erase the stain
that surrounded that room like a murder site
a crime scene.

My father's friend Homer in black leather loafers
eulogized about nights
he and my dad spent in jail
in fancy suits my father designed

for bookies and others on the fringe
"It was important how you looked," Homer said.
"Hollywood. The stars."

I bought creamy satin sandals
with rhinestone studs
for a fairy princess dress,
sexy slinky slippers for a prince.
They sat in a box
on a high shelf
in pitch black night.

I take them out and put them on
like the wicked stepsister.
They have become tight.
But I never wore them!
Throw them out!
But I never wore them!
You'll break your ankle, silly.
You're too old.

I put the pair into the growing pile of
to-be-determined-later.
Put on hold.

7
The month I met my husband,
I bought my first pair of Ivy League loafers
to match new fall colored cords –
to mirror his East Coast
prep schools, Harvard, wholesome.
Sex after:
waxing, shaving, showering,
Makeup, make down, suck in

Hold it
Hold it
Hold it.

The carpetbag sandals from our vacation in London!
Perfect hostess shoes, I thought,
for when we have all those people over –
never worn.
Glittery Indian shoes for weddings
and whirling at all those parties –
never worn.

8
Like my mother,
the floor of her closet
covered in possibilities
for different moods, different careers, a different life.
Espadrilles,
colorful as a Mediterranean beach
bright with bathers.
But not one pair with support
for her arch, her toes, her heel.

Even at eighty, she lives on the edge –
barely dressed, dreaming, drinking
as if immortal.

Even crossing the street
in pouring rain,
no sensible shoes.
Not one pair.
Even as she loses her balance.
Even as she falls.

Even as I fall
into frightening terrain –
remembering my crib
reaching for my mother,
who clung to my father
and the father she never had.

Generation to generation –
slippery genes.
The fear of open space,
where abandonment slips through.
You can't let go enough to live.

9
Am I the same?

Is the DNA so strong
it seeps into my shoes?
Into my closet?
Into my soul?

I thought I would be different, strong
with a spine a mile long.

10
Why did I always dream in shoes?

Saint shoes,
sinner shoes.

Sensible shoes.
Boring, boring, boring.
Does romance have to be in high heels?
Did I eat my mama's mashed up values
thinking I was different?
But hidden in my closet
the same old
bound feet
that cannot run, or jump, or swim,
or save herself from
a bad marriage?

11
Where are my hiking boots, sturdy shoes,
clunkers that save me from
that fate?
Where are the Superman slippers
to make me fly?
The magic galoshes
to save me from the flood?

What do I wear day to day?
Who is loyal?
Tennies.
Where do I feel freedom?
Tennies on trails.

Agile hops from stone to stone
across wide creeks,
down gullies, up switchbacks.
Climb that tree and see for miles.

Calluses, skin, nails
not painted pink acrylic,
but real toes.

No Spanish dancer shoes
with heels too high.
Tennies on the dance floor too.

Almost bare feet
that glide along the beach.
The strong arch
cold surf around my ankles
keeping me awake.

12
Suffice it to say,
I am no longer lost
down that rabbit hole.
I was sitting in a tower of designer boxes –
a pile of shoes
the fairy princess castle
a house of cards.

Throw them out.
Tear down the walls.
Put on your tennies
and run.

FOUND

FIRST FLIGHT

1

I was so afraid to fly, it took me until my forties to fly east of the
Rockies to finally visit my brother. That turbulent landing. That
drop drop drop onto flat cornland. Where I thought for sure,
holding the hand of a nun, no less, in the seat beside me, that
we were about to die. We felt the long long drop – then anoth-
er – grip – then another – grip grip – our hearts pounding. Air
sucked in. The landing so rough. Rape of the plane. Skidding to
a stop. All I could think was, Never again. Never again.

Then I'm on the phone with my brother from a phonebooth in
Chicago. Clutching the receiver. "See what happens when I fly?
It's a plot. It's providence. I'm going to die."

Those first flights were always the same. Down the tube that
led to the plane, stiff shouldered, ready to bolt at the slightest
provocation. Greeted by flight attendants. But it wasn't them I
was interested in. My eyes searchlights. Where is the pilot? Any
dark circles? Redness around the nose – signs of alcohol? I never
fly on the weekend – the rookie flights. Always Monday through
Friday, the nine-to-fiver's, veterans who know what to do, even
in their sleep.

Huddled in my seat, blanket wrapped around me, jacket over my
head, ears plugged up with Chopin on Walkman to help keep
the plane in the air. In turbulence, I scream into the jacket so no
one can hear.

2

Shortly after we are married, my husband convinces me to fly to
Paris. My big transatlantic first. I buy a whole wardrobe before-
hand to match some Parisian image I have in my head. The look
I must attain. The look that will help hold up the plane. Or at
least I'll look good when the plane crashes.

On that night flight to Paris, there is no turbulence. I gaze out
the window at a perpetual sunrise. An orange horizon glows over
water, promising the day ahead. A glimpse of heaven.

At last, I am able to keep my eyes open. While my husband
sleeps, I review the map, chart miles from San Francisco to Paris.
We are almost there.

After we land and climb down an outdated steel airstair to the
tarmac, get into a cab, the driver careening at high speeds to
Ile St. Louis, we check into our hotel. I am about to lie down.
"Don't sleep," my husband says. "Come. Just down the street."

"I can't keep my eyes open," I say, feeling I might go mad with
exhaustion.

"It's the only way to do it."

I follow as he leads the way over cobblestones, across a small
bridge, the river below effervescent in so much light.

"The Seine," he says. "We're almost there."

He stops. "Notre Dame in morning light."

I look up at a mountain of a cathedral — as magnificent as Half

Dome in Yosemite. My eyes soar to the gargoyles at the top and back to the ground. I can't get enough.

I had come across the ocean to a place I never thought I'd be. It is the closest I've come to believing in God since childhood. My soul unfettered. I can do this!

The years and years of lessons with my therapist. Piles and piles of the arithmetic it took me to add two and two. Over and over. Riding the fear. Riding through the fear. Above it. Below it. Alongside it. In it. On it. Being it. No longer losing to it.

Here I am on the other end of the horizon. The real horizon. Across the whole globe.

The bugles called. The gargoyles did my will. They came to me. They sat for me. They soar in my mind even still. The first time I saw Notre Dame, I knew I had become more whole, more me than ever before on that Il St. Louis.

3

My husband and I visit the National Gallery in London at the end of the day when almost everyone has left. We enter a darkened viewing room and sit on a smooth wood bench to view Leonardo da Vinci's *The Virgin of the Rocks* – his Madonna and Child – not expecting anything too wondrous. We are met by a stunning vision: a mother adoring her child – the adoration so real, it is palpable. It includes me. I sit transfixed, like I am the only one in the world who has discovered this mother and child, a small light bulb hanging over us like a moon in the night sky.

I feel, for the first time, what it must be like – this amazing relationship – from both points of view, the child's and the mother's. I sit in that darkened room as if in a church or synagogue, where my dilemma had always been – *if I don't believe in God, what do I do? How do I trust enough to believe in something?* Under the spell of this mother and child, I wonder how, if you missed the bond the first time around with your own mother, then never had a child of your own, how could you ever be whole? Be truly alive? How could you ever trust the world?

That is the moment I understood promiscuity – my mother's, my own. To be held close. That is, in and of itself, the goal of life for people who didn't get it. That is what it's all about – hopping in and out of men's beds, the late nights chasing. A search for the big tit. The breast. The penis. The nurturing. Relentless pursuit of human flesh. But when confronted with a body, all you can do is sexualize it, unable to really make contact. It is so odd, two naked beings in a natural state, trying to be so intimate, yet incapable.

It is all replicating the original impaired bond. The mother holding her child close, and for some reason, her own fear, distrust, sadness, the way she was never held, is passed on to her child. Side by side, unable to look into each other's eyes. Unable to trust. To give. To receive.

MACONDRAY LANE

My husband, who thinks he is Italian, but is really a Jew from Boston, had always wanted to live in San Francisco near North Beach – the Italian District – on a hill with a view of the Bay. We lived in a tree-lined neighborhood in Berkeley. Torn, as I glanced up at my beloved giant cedar in our yard, I said, "But only if we find a place with a garden." Which, I thought, would be impossible in that part of the city.

Our resourceful real estate agent sent us a handwritten note, describing a cottage on Macondray Lane as "The One. It has both a view and greenery. You'll regret it forever if you pass this up." By the time we discovered she sent that note to all her clients, we had already made our decision. I'll never forget following the moving van, which got stuck on the steep hill next to our new home, my husband's Italian Alfa Romeo shadowed beside the van like a duckling next to its mother.

At first, working 24/7, I barely noticed the lane. I spent hours driving in circles looking for a parking place, usually having to pee – while my husband's pet Alfa took up our city-sized garage. Then, I got breast cancer, which was not nearly as traumatic as being laid off. My much younger frat type male colleagues said I'd be too impaired after treatments to do my high power job. "You deserve to rest," they said, lying in wait for an excuse to get rid of the older woman. My own fault for having stayed in a firm that suffered from all the isms: agism, sexism, racism. But a poor crack-in-the-sidewalk kind of kid, I couldn't let go of the money. Then, the final straw: Hillary lost the election to the evil empty suit, and I just about jumped off the Golden Gate Bridge.

After this series of unfortunate events, I questioned my existence.

What am I doing hiking up this steep slope each day like a mountain goat, the wind billowing at god knows what MPH, fog frizzing my blow-dried hair? Why hadn't I become a social worker? A journalist? A folk singer? My list of regrets grew. While my husband, the architect, loved our urban hood, I felt imprisoned by concrete and frequently escaped to Marin to hike and see my therapist – almost begging her to let me move in.

Fast forward to The Pandemic – and the empty suit – we can't leave out the root cause of our failure to nip the pandemic in the bud. A time I wished I believed in God, but had to admit that I did not. After one month sheltering in place, perched high atop the precipice, the world became an online flatland where friends were arranged across the screen like tiny mice – unrecognizable, unhuggable. Everything split in two: BZ and AZ – Before Zoom and After Zoom.

Suffering from too much me with me, I became so nostalgic for BZ, I knew that if I wasn't careful, I would also split in two and slip into old habits of living in fantasy. All those years of therapy down the drain. You need to be more of a be-here-now wise woman, I said to myself. Even a faux Buddhist would be an improvement.

I sat on my deck in meditation pose, pouting, soon distracted by a flock of vividly green and red wild parrots, squawking between trees. I read they were native to Ecuador and Peru. I also read that the San Francisco fog and Mediterranean climate was so rare that Valparaiso, Chile was our closest climate twin. Every day, I walked up and down the brick, cobblestone, and asphalt path overgrown with flowering plum and cherry trees, nasturtiums, rambler roses, English Ivy and Himalaya blackberries that climb the sandstone hill.

I read about the lane and discovered writers, artists, and crafts-men once lived here. Our cottage had been inhabited by a suffra-gette deeply steeped in revolutionary ideals. I started gardening on the plot across from our cottage, wondering if the suffragette had also tilled soil and planted, but figured she'd probably been too busy organizing the California Communist Party. It was up to me to discover what would grow next to wild thickets and primordial tree-ferns. I experimented with camellias, hydrangeas, even fuchsias and Chinese lanterns.

One day, I looked up and spied an Atlantic cedar alongside ber-ried Cotoneasters – the cherry-headed bird's favorites. I stroked the cedar's bark and breathed in its oxygen – loving this urban tree just as much as my old cedar tree in Berkeley and the trees on trails in Marin.

I read Armistead Maupin's *Tales of the City* and began to un-derstand the characters in a new way – the rich fabric of life on that fictional lane. And here I live on the real lane, where I pass young people strolling hand-in-hand. Kindred spirits in search of free selves, climbing steep steps to view the Bay, breathe in sea salt air, listen to late afternoon and evening winds whip over the hill, seals barking, fog horns on dark, soupy nights – leading ships through the Golden Gate – so that we can all feel safe and cozy in our beds.

It came to me how fortunate I was to be part of this exotic secret world and its history. To live on this lane that invites, accepts, and loves anything wild and alive in this world. Any plant or bird or coyote or human being. Any democratic idea. Any con-stellation of stars. The lane that loves the universe.

ROMANTIC LOVE

At sixteen, nineteen, twenty-nine,
even thirty-five,
yearning,
almost like grief,
compelled by an undertow.
So out of control I couldn't catch my breath.

At home with thorns and scratches –
wanting to win a war.
Chasing dreams and stories,
promises that were never kept.
Clawing for attention,
the kind you only miss
when you haven't been loved enough.

The other person always
a projection
with a barely human outline.

Parched and dry inside
for someone as young as I was,
fear had shut me down.

In clarity of later years,
I discovered the boys that came to me
in unexpected moments were
not the major players.

But the few who were kind –
who had smiles with softer edges
who were unsure of themselves,

even awkward or shy –
unpolished gemstones
that later glowed in the dark.

Romantic love
no longer elusive, like a mirage –
something just around the corner
something I dreamt about.

But boys with whom I had
brief encounters –
respites in between long battles
that got me through hollow fear
that made it possible
to survive.

Buoys.

Like peppermint tea
with honey.
Sitting on the chaise lounge
on my sunny deck
surrounded by lavender,
where I am safe
because I made it through
because I worked so hard
because I now know I deserved
to be loved.

All these years later
I can finally feel the love
that happened long ago.

It is like an old Bob Dylan song –
    grounding, brilliant,
    wholesome, unabashed, fierce,
    natural, nostalgic, flirtatious,
    summery, vulnerable,
    intelligent, creative,
    sexy, quiet, real, free
    fun to dance to
    and laugh with.
    Kindred spirits.

I remember someone saying,
"You always feel young inside,"
but I never felt young
until now.

WE ARE ALL COYOTES

FRIENDSHIP

We walk
in worn tennis shoes and visors,
fast paced, wide awake,
slow going, groggy.

We talk
intelligently, wisely
stupidly, unconsciously –
honesty in whatever form it takes.

We listen to
muted sounds in sea salt fog;
headlong winds from a cold front,
daring us to push further.
A finch's confident whistle,
hoots from the owl we never see,
high up in the tallest eucalyptus tree.
A mournful coyote clan's
holy howls.
A fading way of life.

All the while we
keep our footing on the path –
puddles in winter
slip slide dirt in summer,
lush grass,
growing almost to our shoulders in spring.

We watch
as everything blends perfectly into everything else.
Deer at sunset,

nonchalantly munching as we pass,
cottontails scurrying across the path.
A wolf pup's carefree zigzag in the distance,
a colony of grebes splashing in the lagoon –
tails up as they dive for dinner.
The solitary white egret
almost hidden on the far edge
of the reeded pond.

Our halfway point: the cove
where we stop,
survey the horizon –
which on any given day becomes
possibility, eternity,
monotony, dead ends.

Where last winter's wild currents
carved a sandbar
around which two fast rivers
ran the beach.
Spring tides
carried back the sand,
now perfectly even
from cliff to shore.
We sit on the beach
reminded of
impermanence, continuity.

As we walk back,
our voices
rise loud, true
fall lost, muddled.

We answer
each other, ourselves
gently, gracefully, awkwardly
finding our voices
fueling our hearts –
honesty in whatever form it takes.

THE EIGHT O'CLOCK HOWL

Every evening we howl.

To thank the ones in danger's way
the ones who stay up late
the ones who never sleep
the ones who get up before dawn.

And because we don't want to be alone.

Every evening we howl.

to say we're sorry
to say we're sad
to say from the deepest place
we never thought it would get this bad.

Every evening we howl.

Or sing or clap or bang
or whoop or hoot or hiss
or scream or swear or sigh.

Thanking you while worrying
will there ever be an end?

Howling for the aching ones
the ones who cannot breathe.
Howling for the oxygen
the forests we've aggrieved.
Howling for the wolves we were
those who have been deceived.

We howl aloud the grief of freedom passing.

Howling for the lives we've lost,
for our decency and pride.
Aching for the time before
when we didn't have to hide

from the pain of our nation's turbulence,
rushing in like a fast tide.
We rebel against the signs of freedom passing.

Every night we howl,
drawing up the courage
from the well that's deep inside –
that deepest place that says "Enough!
You cannot have our pride."

Dante had proclaimed
nine circles of hell.
This child king has sunk
so many layers deeper –
for that he shall be blamed.

He's taken our nation's innocence.
The young have become the old
"Get up! Get up!" the children scream.
They've never been so bold.

They're howling from the canyons,
the cities and the coasts.
They're protesting with Fonda, with Thunberg,

running with Estes' wolves –
channeling Ginsburg.

We are all coyotes.

AT THE END OF MY WALK

This is what I come for.
In the sound of my steps,
to forget, to remember,
to lose, then find myself.

The familiar valley always pulls me in.
Following the trail in late afternoon,
my feet clomp on gravel, then dirt.
With each step away
from the parking lot
my mind unclenches.

Away from day to day:
    freeways, clocks, net worth,
    designer labels, political polarization,
    the destruction of our planet,
    starving children, plagues, wars,
    nuclear stockpiles, the fear of Armageddon.
    religious arguments, disappearing values of peace,
    freedom. A president wreaking wrath on our democracy.

Baby green grass from last week's rain
asserts itself through dry fall foliage
like a calf learning to walk,
wobbly but strong.
So ready to live.

My eyes slowly adjust,
opening slowly as colors deepen.
So many greens on either side
of the brown path before me,
like an elegant canvas.

Faster paced, into a rhythm,
breath and heart strong,
I climb higher and higher,
crisscrossing the steep slope
to the overlook,
the shell shaped cove far below.
Eyes wide at the expanse of coastline
to the north,
to the south,
blue grey ocean
as far as I can see
to the west.

Reciting childhood innocence:
>   *I can see so wide*
>   *Rivers and trees and mountains and all*
>   *Over the countryside...*

Hiking back down,
I stop at the lagoon
where grebes glide in elegant formation
alongside pampas grass
like bright green head-dresses.

Reaching the beach,
I relax on grainy sand,
propped by my down jacket against
the bottom of the cliff.
The surf pounds as waves spray.
I breathe in sea salt ions
as the incoming tide approaches
with the cool hiss of natural secrets.

This is where I reflect
on a time when I couldn't lean back.
Any ability I have
to trust myself or others,
even for a moment,
is the result of years of excavation,
examining each layer of my geography,
the relief map of my interior
that gave me the compass
that had eluded me all my life.

In the process of understanding,
I am always forgetting.
This is how the unconscious works:
you unearth things –
they come into the light.
Then you go dark awhile.

At the beginning, more lost.
Later, more found.

Developing trust is like
the heart and mind
learning to speak a new language.
How many times did I doubt,
unsure if I would ever change.

Then an insight
would rush in
like this tide –
proof I'd traveled far.

At the end of my walk,
the sun about to go down
owls *who-who* from tall eucalyptus.
I re-enter the parking lot
to the howl of coyotes –
kindred spirits.
I take that as a sign
that I have, at long last,
joined the human race.

SONGBIRD

"Magic is believing in yourself..."

Watching Yehudi Menuhin play Bach,
the notes soared,
then landed on a tree branch, then soared again.
I was swaddled in the warm timbre of the wood
as I remembered the songbird alighting
tree-to-tree on the Bear Valley Trail.

I could hear the violin because of Olema,
where I had recently stayed and reclaimed
the younger part of myself
so frozen back then
in years growing up in Stinson and Bolinas.

Dormant forty years, I had finally visited unafraid,
and came alive
in the overpowering urge to run
in cold surf at Stinson,
alongside flocks of grebes feeding along the shoreline,
seagulls circling overhead,
excited at finding a sand dollar.

The sound of waves filling my head –
all chatter gone.
The crisscross waves at the end of the sandspit
where the tide rushed out
and wet sand along the channel calved
like tiny glaciers into rushing water,
melting into the sea along with old ghosts.

The dilapidated shed in Bolinas
where I had lost my innocence
transformed into a newly painted farmhouse
with a giant peace sign.

Morning frost brought the excitement of Christmas morning –
at dusk, I was enchanted by deer and birds feeding along Bear
Valley Trail.
At night, surprised at a sky of stars.

Without fear, able to see in color,
feel in rainbows.
Fragments of the past
coming together like a giant puzzle.

CLAUDIA COLE BLUHM – BIO

I grew up in a working class neighborhood in San Francisco. My diary, Sarah, became my best friend. Life in the city filled her pages: fog racing over Twin Peaks each afternoon; my Gram, brother and I dipping jelly doughnuts into milked-down coffee on Saturday mornings; our father, nicknamed Harry the Horse, driving up in his T-bird convertible, a Camel cigarette perpetually hanging from his mouth. Our glamorous blonde *shiksa* mother, Bunny, practicing for acting auditions. Why had the Catholic kids next-door made fun of our father's "big Jewish nose"? Why didn't I have a rosary to save my family from hell and the fire that burned forever? What was Gram saying as she crooned in Yiddish with a worried look upon her face? When we moved to the suburbs, then out to Stinson Beach and Bolinas, I kept on writing to answer those questions and never stopped.

With gratitude to teachers: Diane O'Hehir and Sheila Ballantyne at Mills College; Michael Ruben, Diane Frank at SF State University; Dan Coshnear at UC Berkeley; Anne Lamott, Elizabeth George, Adair Lara at Book Passage. The Bird by Birds in perpetuity: Amy Beauchamp, Terri Tate, Margit Liesche, Mary Cone, Caiti Collins. Writing partner Elizabeth Kert. Writers: Nancy Taforo-Murphy, Akasha Halsey, Amy Metzenbaum, Annie Graham, Thelma Tucker, Elinor Gale, Steve Nelson. Diane Frank for editing. Nan Cassady & Susan Arndt for photos. Abby Stricker for always listening. Patricia Frisch for my transformative journey. Chef husband Bob for amazing meals.

Grateful acknowledgement is made to the editors of the following publications: "The Eight O'clock Howl" appears in The Haight Ashbury Literary Journal; "Liberty Street" appears in Fog and Light: San Francisco through the Eyes of the Poets Who Live Here published by Blue Light Press; "Summer in the City" appears in Pandemic Puzzle Poems published by Blue Light Press, also in When the World Lost Its Balance published by Two Tails Publishing.

CPSIA information can be obtained
at www.ICGtesting.com
Printed in the USA
LVHW020749210221
679520LV00006B/747